Flowers

for

Cake Decorating

with Modelling Tools

Sixteen different species of moulded Australian native flowers make up the wired sprays for a three-leaf-clover shaped wedding cake

Flowers

for

Cake Decorating

with Modelling Tools

Caroline Matthias
and
Barbara Walter

ROBERT HALE • LONDON

Front cover: A wired spray of brilliantly coloured Australian native flowers
Back cover: Single roses

Photography
Dora Evans AFIAP, AAPS, ESAPS
Brian Walter LAPS

Technical Adviser
John Meredith OAM

First published in Great Britain 1992

ISBN 0 7090 4723 1

Robert Hale Limited
Clerkenwell House
Clerkenwell Green
London ECIR OHT

Printed in Hong Kong

Contents

Index of Flowers

Traditional

Australian Native

Introduction

This book is designed to show just how quick, easy and inexpensive it is to make beautiful sugar flowers. We demonstrate more than sixty flowers, made using just a set of modelling tools. This method eliminates the expense of a lot of the special equipment and cutters generally used to make sugar flowers. Modelling tools, we feel, allow greater freedom to the cake decorator to achieve more natural-looking flowers.

We begin with detailed step-by-step instructions, each step photographically illustrated, for the hyacinth, single daisy, buttercup, daffodil, orchid, rose, snowdrop and carnation. Once you have mastered the techniques used in these flowers, you can move on to the advanced sections on traditional flowers and Australian native flowers.

We would like to acknowledge the early encouragement of John Meredith and his invaluable advice during the writing, without which this book would not have made it to print.

We were fortunate to have Barbara's husband Brian to do the colour photography for the book and our good friend Dora Evans to do the black and white photography. To our husbands and families who contributed so much in so many ways, many thanks.

Caroline Matthias
Barbara Walter

Equipment

Set of Caroline's Modelling Tools.*
Non-stick board and rolling pin.
Moulding stick, curler or roller pin, toothpick, scissors, cornflour (or arrowroot or potato flour), covered wire, wire cutters, Parafilm or flower tape, stamens, brushes, egg-white or water and a sponge.

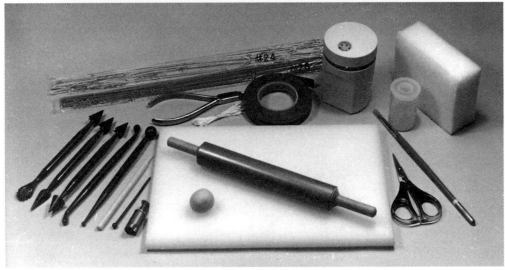

---

*Caroline's Modelling Tools are available from most cake decorating shops, or from Caroline's Sugar Art Services, 42 Quick Road, Mitchell Park, South Australia 5043 and Lincoln House, 198 Desborough Road, High Wycombe, Bucks HP112 Q4, England.

Moulding Paste Recipe

Ingredients

500 g Pettinice plastic icing
1 teaspoon gum tragacanth
1 teaspoon pure albumen powder or ½ teaspoon egg-white
½ teaspoon *grated* Copha (white vegetable fat). DO NOT MELT.

Knead with icing sugar, not cornflour.
Store in an airtight container and leave for 24 hours at room temperature before using.
The paste can be frozen after 24 hours in smaller pieces if desired.
If using egg white as a binding agent, instead of pure albumen, knead the gum tragacanth through the icing thoroughly before adding the egg white.
Pure albumen and gum tragacanth can be added together, however.

Hints
For winter or humid climates, add 1 teaspoon gelatine dissolved in 2 teaspoons *luke*warm water. Place dissolved gelatine mixture over *hot* water, add icing sugar until it reaches a kneading consistency, then add to already prepared moulding paste and knead thoroughly.

Note
All the flowers in this book were made from this recipe, but any moulding paste is suitable.

Glossary

Flatten   Gently press the petal between finger and thumb.
Frill   Hold cone between thumb and finger and using No.5 tool, stroke-frill (tease) edge of cone back over side of finger.
Neaten back   Use scissors to remove any excess paste at base of flower. Neaten base by fingering.
Pinch   Gently pinch the tip of the petal to a fine point.

Round edge   With finger, gently round off corners of square petal section.
Stretch   Gently ease petal along thumb with index finger. Use cornflour or arrowroot to prevent sticking.
Thin out   Roll petals over finger with a curling pin, toothpick or moulding stick.

The Modelling Tools— the numbering system

The basic types of flowers which can be made with the modelling tools are described in a step-by-step manner in the following section of this book.

The flowers appearing in the colour pages, together with their relevant descriptions, should enable the reader to make the flowers described by referring back to the relevant step-by-step description

The numbers in brackets after the flower-name heading denote which tools are used for the flower described.

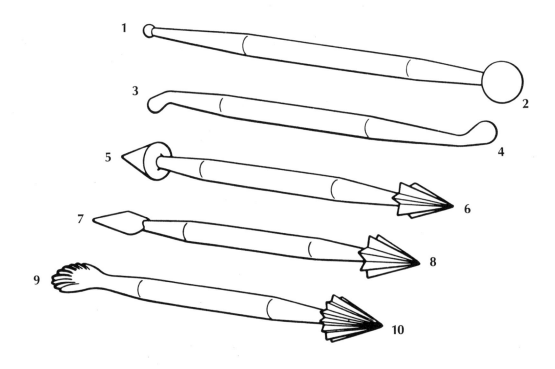

To Start With

All flowers begin with an appropriately sized piece of paste, which is then formed into a cone, a cigar shape or a 'starter' on wire.

The cone or cigar shapes are formed prior to inserting the recommended tool into the centre.

The starter is a piece of hooked wire with its hook covered with a very small piece of moulding paste. Make it into a very small bud and allow to dry.

Important

The flowers in this book are made on the wire stems used in wired sprays. These sprays of flowers are attached to the cake with a small amount of royal icing and can be easily removed and kept.

NEVER PUSH WIRES INTO A CAKE.

From left to right, these pieces of paste are: 1, medium-sized cigar shape; 2, medium cone; 3, large ball; 4, medium ball; 5, small ball; 6, very small ball (starter); 7, large cone (in fingers)

This moulded swan makes a lovely cake top for birthday, wedding or christening cakes.
Here it has been filled with small roses, hyacinths and violets

Step-by-Step Flower Instructions

Hyacinth (6)(7)

Plates 1 and 30

A: With a small piece of moulding paste form a cone. Insert (6) tool into cone, making sure that paste is formed evenly around tool.

B: With scissors cut about one-third of the way towards the centre along each mark.

Gently STRETCH each petal section by easing along with index finger (using cornflour or arrowroot to prevent sticking).

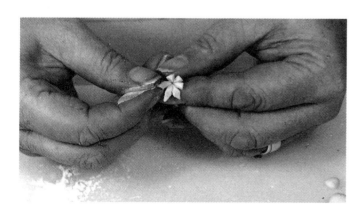

C: PINCH the very tip of the petal to a fine point.

Gently PRESS and FLATTEN the tip of the petal between index finger and thumb to remove any mark from pinching (this prevents paste from splitting when thinning out petal).

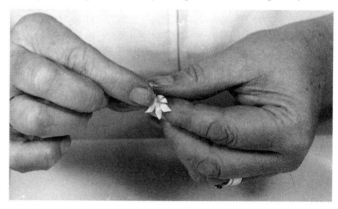

D: Gently THIN each petal by using a toothpick with a side-to-side rolling action.

E: Vein centre of each petal with (7) tool.

F: Insert moistened stamen.

Gently curl the outer section of each petal backwards.

NEATEN back of flower by cutting off excess paste with scissors and neatening with fingers.

Single Daisy (8 or 10)(5)

Plates 2 and 1

Centre Colour some semolina by adding lemon-yellow petal dust and shaking it in a sealed container.

Take a small piece of yellow paste and form a cone. Insert a moistened, hooked wire into pointed end. When dry, dip top in egg white and then into prepared semolina.

Petals

A: Using a slightly larger piece of paste than for the centre, form a cone and insert (8) or (10) tool.

B: Mark petals with (8) or (10) tool.

C: Cut each petal with scissors.

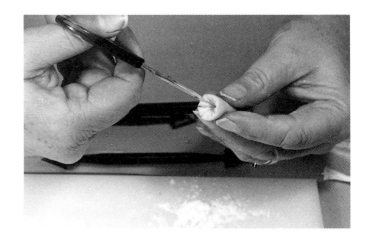

14

D: STRETCH petals out.

E: PINCH each petal to a point and smooth out.

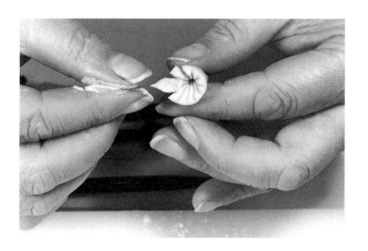

F: THIN each petal with a rolling action of moulding stick.

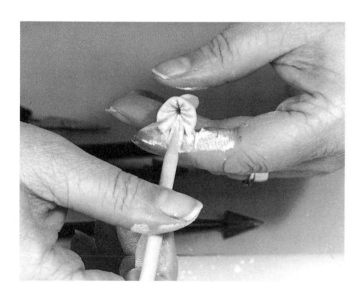

G: Vein petal with (8) or (10) tool by rolling from side to side.

H: Open up centre with (5) tool.

I: Take moistened prepared centre...

J: ...and insert through the flower.

K: NEATEN back with scissors.

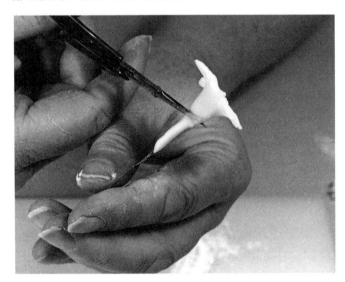

Buttercup (10) (4)

Plate 1

A: Pre-tape 11 or 12 stamen stems to a wire.
Form a cone and using (10) tool cut alternate markings.
FLATTEN and ROUND petals.
Press (10) tool into centre again for natural veining.

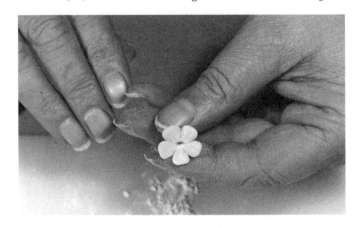

B: With a (4) tool and using a circular motion form a cup in each petal.

C: Moisten prepared wired stamens and insert through centre of flower.
NEATEN back.

Daffodil (5) (1) (6) (7)

Plate 3

Trumpet section

A: Tape 3 yellow stamens to a wire stem.

With a large piece of lemon modelling paste form a cone and open out centre with a (5) plain cone tool.

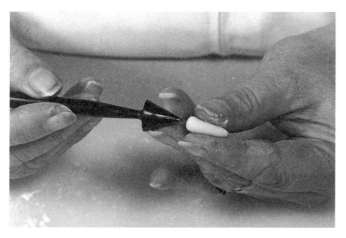

B: With (5) tool or curler pin, FRILL edge of trumpet...

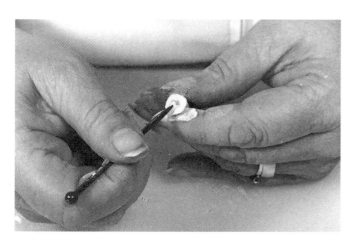

C: ...by stroke-frilling over edge of finger.

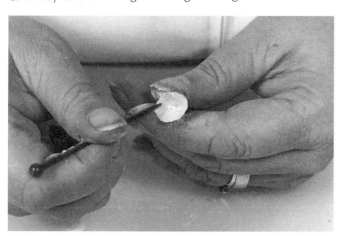

D: With small ball tool (1)...

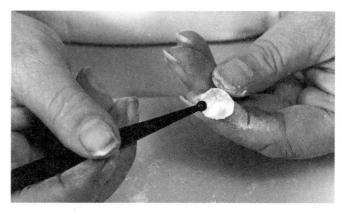

E: ...open out bottom of trumpet.

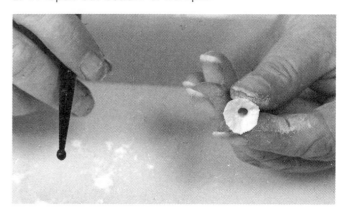

Petal section

F: With a large piece of moulding paste form a cone and mark with (6) tool. Cut alternate markings deeply and stretch each section quite long.

PINCH, POINT and FLATTEN each petal. Thin each petal with a modelling stick along full length and vein centre with V tool (7).

Repeat procedure. Assemble both parts together to form a symmetrical 6-petal section.

G: With plain cone tool (5) form a shallow cone in centre of petal section.

Moisten and assemble trumpet into petal section.

H: Moisten stem and insert through centre until stamens are level with trumpet or slightly below.

NEATEN back.

Leave to dry before colouring, if necessary.

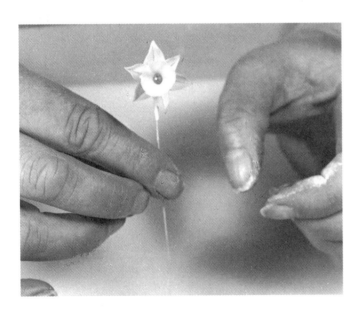

Pattern for orchid throat

Orchid (10) (1)

Plates 4, 1 and 26

Tongue

A: Attach a small elongated teardrop-shaped paste section to a wire stem, and cup it with the small ball tool (1).

Leave to dry.

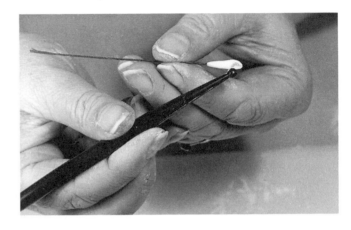

Throat

B: Roll out moulding paste.

C: Cut out throat with cutter or pattern.

(For the throats of larger orchids make the paste thicker and roll again after cutting out.)

D: Use curler pin to frill edge and (10) tool to vein throat.

G: With (1) tool roll the back petal forward.

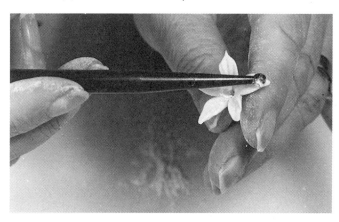

E: Moisten edge of throat and wrap around the pre-made tongue section on wire.

Tip back top section of throat.

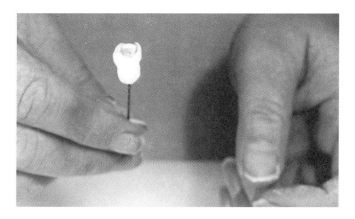

H: Moisten pre-made throat section and thread through the centre.

Curve the top central petal further forwards.

Twist the two side petals slightly.

Petals

F: Form a cone of moulding paste and mark with (10) tool.

Cut deeply along alternate markings.

Ease between thumb and forefinger and STRETCH petals.

PINCH petals to a point and then smooth each one out.

Use modelling stick to widen petals and (10) tool to vein each petal.

A finished spray of orchids

19

Rose (10) (6) (5) (3) (1)

Plates 1, 5, 17, 30, 37, 38 and 39

A: Make a small starter (see p.11) on a piece of wire. Form a cone of moulding paste and mark with (6) tool. Cut on alternate markings.

B: STRETCH and ROUND each of the three petals.

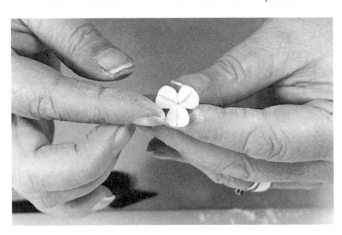

C: Thin petals by using modelling stick with a side-to-side and pivoting action over the finger.
Cut each petal division slightly deeper.

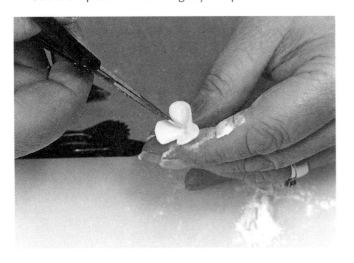

D: Moisten the starter piece on the wire and place through the centre of the three petals.

E: Moisten the inside leading edge of each petal.

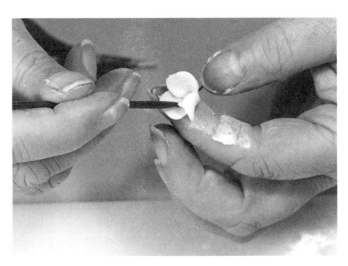

F: Assemble with outside edge of the adjoining petal forming a symmetrical pattern.

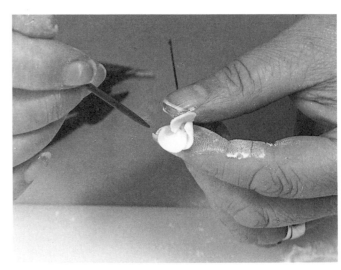

G: Smooth to a neat finish.
   NEATEN back.

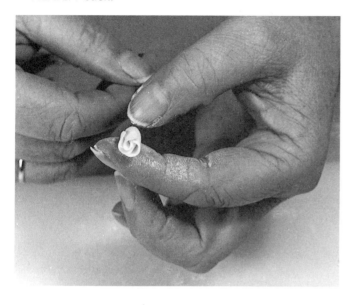

H: For the next round of petals, repeat the procedure, i.e. form, cut, stretch and round.

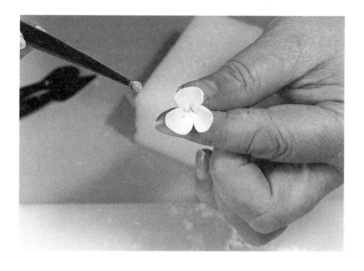

I: Place petals upside down on sponge foam.

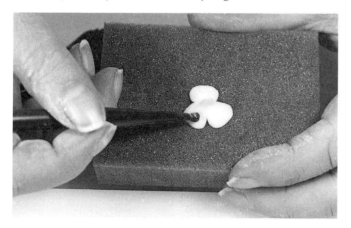

J: Using tool (1), bounce it 2-3 times on back of each petal.

K: With (5) tool form shallow cone in centre of round. Moisten already made centre and partway up each petal and assemble,...

L: ...pushing moistened stem through the new round of petals and making sure back is secure before tipping outer edges of petals back slightly.
   NEATEN back.

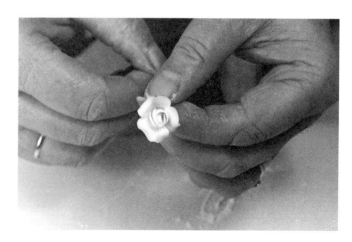

M: For a third round of petals, use (10) tool to form cone from a larger piece of paste, making shallow cuts on alternate markings.

Repeat as before. Petals must be made wider at bottom so that they will overlap when assembled.

Use (3) tool to deepen centre and assemble as before.

Tip petals backwards slightly. NEATEN back.

Form a fourth cone from a larger piece of paste and with (6) tool cut each marking shape and work as before (but tip one side of petal over more than the other).

Make sure with each successive build-up of petals that each petal is centred on the joins of the petals of the previous build-up.

For a rosebud use first round of three petals only.

For a small rose use two rounds of petals.

For a medium rose use three rounds of petals.

Rose Calyx (10) (3) (7)

Form a small cone from green paste.

Using (10) tool and cutting alternate markings, STRETCH, PINCH and FLATTEN each section.

Use (10) tool to vein each petal and make a small cut on some of the petals.

Use (3) tool to form hollow in centre; moisten centre and assemble previously dried and coloured flower.

Tip over calyx tips if necessary.

Mark lower section of calyx with edge of (7) tool to form bulb.

Snowdrop (6) (1)

Plate 6

A: Form small piece of white paste into a cone and mark with (6) tool.

Cut each marking, forming six petals.

Pinch petals to a point and smooth pinch marks.

Thin cone with roller pin or toothpick on inside of finger.

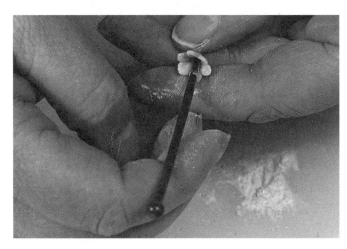

B: With (1) tool and a stroking action downwards cup petals over inside of finger.

C: Insert a moistened yellow stamen in centre.

When dry, paint a green dot on the tip of each petal, inside and outside, and near the base.

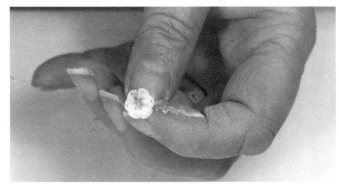

Carnation (5) (10)

Plate 7

A: Make a small starter on a wire and allow to dry.

Take a medium-sized piece of paste and form a cone with the (5) tool.

Using the (5) tool, FRILL edge of cone by stroke-frilling (teasing) over finger. This frill should be very fine.

B: Moisten base of frill, insert starter and wrap frill around to form centre of carnation.

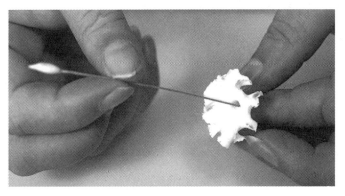

C: NEATEN back by cutting off excess paste and fingering.

Take another, slightly larger, piece of paste, form a cone and with (5) tool frill the edge by stroke-frilling over finger as in step A.

D: Using (5) tool, open up centre, moisten and insert first stage.

Wrap frill around and NEATEN back.

Repeat steps C and D if a larger carnation is needed.

For a more realistic carnation put 4 or 5 cuts in the cone of the final row before frilling. This gives the effect of petals.

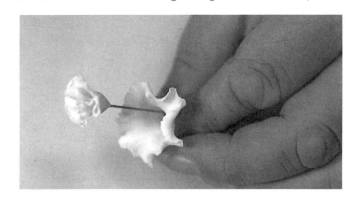

Carnation Calyx (5) (10)

A: Take a piece of green paste and form a cone using the (10) tool. Cut on alternate markings. Pinch, flatten and thin.

Open up calyx with the (5) tool and add to carnation flower.

NEATEN back.

B: With scissors, make 5 small snips around base of calyx for a realistic finish.

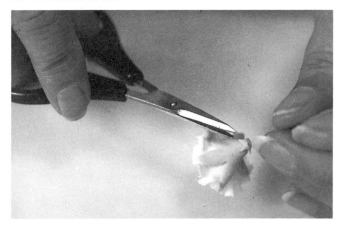

A piped lace bell cake top filled with primroses and bouvardia

Traditional Flowers

Agapanthus (6) (7)

Plates 8 and 9

1. Tape 5 fine white stamens and 1 thicker stamen (a little longer than the rest) to a wire stem.
2. Make a medium-sized cone of white or pale blue paste with the (6) tool.
3. Make long cuts on each marking.
4. Stretch and pinch each petal.
5. Thin each petal with moulding stick on inside of finger.
6. Mark a vein down the centre of each petal with the (7) tool.
7. Moisten stamens and insert into centre. Neaten back.
8. Colour each stamen tip an ochre colour.

Apple Blossom (10) (4)

Plates 6 and 10

This flower can be made quite small if used for filler flowers in an arrangement, or a little larger if used as focal flowers.

1. Prepare 8 or 9 pale pink stamen stems with red-painted tips taped to a single wire stem.
2. With a medium piece of paste form a cone, mark with (10) tool and cut on alternate marks with scissors.
3. Flatten and round petals.
4. Thin each petal with a moulding stick over side of index finger.
5. With a (4) tool, using a circular motion, form a 'cup' of each petal, tilting slightly inwards.
6. Moisten prepared wired stamens and insert through centre, neaten back.

Blossoms may also be made with six petals using a (6) tool.

Bluebell (English) (6) (1)

1. Tape three yellow stamens to wire stem.
2. Proceed the same as for hyacinth (pages 13-14), but before inserting stamens, use (1) ball tool in centre to form bell shape.
3. When dry, paint dark blue with liquid colour diluted with spirits.

Bougainvillea (5) (6) (10)

Plate 11

Centre
1. From a tiny piece of moulding paste make a very fine cigar shape 2 cm long.
2. With the (5) tool make a tiny hole in the top and place on a very fine piece of wire.
3. Repeat once.
4. Take a slightly larger piece of paste, form a cigar shape and mark one end with the (10) tool.
5. With scissors, put a very shallow cut on each marking, forming a very small flower. Place on a fine wire.
6. These 3 fine wires are then taped to a stronger piece of wire to form the centre.

Flower

1. Make a medium-sized cone using the (6) tool and cut on alternate markings to form 3 brads (petals.)
2. Stretch, pinch and thin petals.
3. Vein each petal, inside and out, with veins more prominent on the outside.
4. With toothpick, on the side of finger or sponge, run along the outside centre vein to make petals concave.
5. Moisten wire of centre and pull through petals. Neaten back.
6. Colour as desired with petal dust or liquid colour diluted with spirits.

Bouvardia (8)

Plates 12 and 26

1. With very small amount of paste form cone. Mark with (8) tool and make short cuts on alternate markings.
2. Pinch petals to a fine point and smooth pinch marks. Thin with curler pin with rolling action on side of finger.
3. Insert moistened stamen down into centre of flower. Neaten back.

Bud is long, bulbous at tip.

Left to right: Boronia (page 53), daphne (page 29), bouvardia (above) and lilac (page 32)

Camellia No. 1 (6) (4)

Plate 14

1. Begin by making the same centre section as for a rose (page 20).
2. Form a medium-sized cone section and mark with a (6) tool.

3. Make six short cuts with scissors.
4. Flatten petals and round edges, then thin with moulding stick.
5. Gently dish the back of each petal on a foam block with a (4) tool.
6. Moisten 'rose' centre and stem, and assemble.
7. Make another two rows of six petals, each one slightly larger than the one before, and assemble.
8. Make sure that the centre of each petal aligns with the joint line of the preceding row of petals.

Camellia No. 2 (6) (4)

1. Tape about 20 yellow stamens to a wire stem.
2. Form a medium-sized cone and mark with (6) tool.
3. Make six short cuts with scissors.
4. Gently dish the back of each petal on a foam block with a (4) tool.
5. Moisten stem and assemble.
6. Make another three rows of petals, each row slightly larger than the one before, and assemble.
7. Make sure that the centre of each petal aligns with the joint line of the preceding row of petals.

Carolina Yellow Jessamine (10) (5)

Plate 13

1. Tape 3 yellow stamens to a wire stem.
2. Make a medium-sized cone of lemon-yellow moulding paste with the (10) tool.
3. Make short cuts on alternate markings for 5 petals.
4. Flatten and round petals.
5. Thin each petal with moulding stick over finger to give petal natural movement.
6. Open up centre with moulding stick or (5) tool to make a tube-shaped flower.
7. Moisten stamens and insert into centre. Neaten back.
8. Dust with lemon-yellow petal dust.

Buds are long and slim.

Chrysanthemum (6) (8) (10)

Plate 13

A chrysanthemum is made in a similar manner to a dahlia (see next column), with one major difference. Each petal section is cut in two before the petal is shaped. The last row of petals is curved backwards slightly.

Cyclamen (10) (5)

Plate 15

Centre
1. Prepare 5 stamen stems, one a little longer than the others, and tape to wire stem.

2. Take a tiny piece of moulding paste and secure around taped area. Take tweezers and pinch 5 even lines around moulding paste. Allow to dry.

Flower
1. Take a large piece of moulding paste and form a cone using the (10) tool.
2. Cut on alternate markings, making 5 petals.
3. Stretch petals and thin with moulding stick.
4. With the (5) tool, frill around each petal with a teasing action.
5. Open centre with (5) tool.
6. Moisten back of previously prepared centre piece and pull through. Neaten back.
7. Turn petals down along stem; pinch base of petals around centre hollow, using finger and thumb.
8. Using tweezers, grip wire just behind neatened back and bend at 90° between any two petals.
9. Dust centre with burgundy petal dust.

For a non-frilled cyclamen, follow the same instructions, but omit frilling of petals (step 4).

Dahlia—Petticoat (8) (7) (5)

1. Prepare a centre on wire in the same way as for a daisy (see page 14) and allow to dry.
2. Form a medium cone on an (8) tool, and cut each marking.
3. Stretch and pinch each petal, then thin with a moulding stick.
4. Vein each petal with the centre of the (7) tool—this makes the petals slightly concave.
5. Open the centre of the flower with a (5) tool.

On the left a spray of the petticoat dahlia (above); on the right apple blossom (page 25)

27

6. Moisten the centre and stem and place in flower.
7. Form two more rows of petals in a similar manner with (8) tool, remembering to alternate each row of petals.

Dahlia—Pom-pom (6) (3 or 4) (8) (10)

1. Attach a small ball of icing to a piece of wire and allow to dry.
2. Form a medium cone from a medium-sized piece of paste, mark with a (6) tool and cut each mark.
3. Pinch each petal and thin with a moulding stick.
4. With a (3) tool cup each petal on inside of finger, easing each petal inward.
5. Moisten wire stem and ball and assemble into petal section, wrapping the petals around the ball section.
6. With a slightly larger piece of paste make a second petal section, as above.
7. Moisten centre and assemble.
8. Make another two petal sections using an (8) tool, making one slightly larger than the other.
9. Assemble both petal sections.
10. Make another two petal sections using a (10) tool for marking and a (4) tool for cupping.

11. Assemble final two petal sections.
12. Colour as required.

Daisy—Double (8) (1) (5)

Plate 16

1. Prepare a daisy centre (see page 14).
2. Form a medium cone, insert the (8) tool and cut each marking for 8 petals.
3. Stretch and pinch each petal.
4. Cut each petal in half, making 16 petals.
5. Thin each petal with a moulding stick.
6. Use the (1) tool to give natural movement to petals.
7. Moisten daisy centre and insert into flower. Neaten back.
8. Make a second row of same-size petals; using (5) tool, open the centre of this row a little.
9. Insert previous petals and centre.

Daisy—Michaelmas (5)

1. Roll tiny piece of yellow paste into a ball and attach to a moistened hooked wire.

An arrangement featuring the Michaelmas daisy (above), daffodils (page 17) and jonquils (page 32)

2. Form a very small piece of white paste into a cone.
3. Use (5) cone tool on the inside of finger until shell is very fine, and with scissors cut many closely spaced petals.
4. Assemble moistened stem into centre of flower.

Daphne (8)

1. With a tiny piece of pink paste form cone. Mark with (8) tool and cut on alternate markings.
2. Pinch petals to a fine point and smooth pinch marks. With curler pin and inside of finger, thin each petal with rolling action.
3. Insert single moistened stamen right down into flower. Paint back of flower with burgundy colour.

Dianthus (Sweet William) (5) (10)

Plate 17

1. Tape 5 short stamen cottons to a fine wire stem.
2. Make a medium-sized cone with (10) tool.
3. Cut on alternate markings, making 5 shallow petals.
4. With (5) tool, frill edge of each petal by stroke-frilling (teasing) over edge of finger.
5. Moisten stamens and pull through centre.
6. Neaten back.
7. When dry, paint with liquid food colour (pink or burgundy).

English Lavender (5) (8)

Plate 18

Bud
1. With a very tiny piece of moulding paste, form a cigar shape.
2. With (5) tool, slightly open centre and place on a moistened, fine wire. Allow to dry.
3. Take a very tiny piece of green moulding paste and form a cigar shape once again.
4. With (5) tool open centre up, moisten and pull previously dried bud through, leaving 0.5 cm protruding.

Flower
1. With a very small piece of lavender coloured moulding paste, form a cone and mark with (10) tool.
2. Cut 3 petals on alternate markings, leaving 4 markings to form one larger petal.

3. Thin the 4 petals out on front of finger with the curler pin, moisten centre and pull a moistened wire through.
4. Tilt flower forward as for violet (page 51), but leaving longer petal at top.

Forget-me-not (10)

Plate 19

1. Form cone from tiny piece of blue paste, mark with (10) tool and cut alternate markings.
2. Flatten petals and round edges.
3. Place tool back in centre to produce natural veining.
4. Insert small moistened yellow stamen in centre, neaten back.

Freesia (6) (3)

1. Prepare 3 stamens taped to wire stem.
2. Proceed the same as for Christmas bell (page 53), although the flower is more trumpet-shaped.
3. Use (3) tool to curve petals inward.
4. Place moistened prepared stamens into centre. Neaten back.

Fuchsia, Single (8) (7) (5)

Plate 20

Tape 8 stamens 3 cm long and 1 stamen 5 cm long to a wire stem.

Centre section
1. Form a cone from medium-sized, suitably coloured paste and mark with (8) tool.

2. Cut on alternate marks for four petals and stretch to form the longer rounded petals of the central part of flower. Thin with moulding stick on centre of finger.
3. Cut petals deeper and fold in towards centre so that each petal has one edge in front and one edge behind the adjacent petals in a symmetrical pattern.
4. Moisten stem and insert through centre of 'tube' of petals.

Back petal section
1. Form a cone from a medium-sized piece of suitably coloured paste and mark with (8) tool.
2. Cut alternate markings, pinch, ease to fairly long section. Thin out.
3. Vein down centre with (7) tool.
4. Form shallow cone in centre with (5) tool. Moisten centre and stem and assemble. Fold petals back slightly. Mould tiny green bud and place on back.

On the left, single fuchsias; on the right, double fuchsias

Fuchsia, Double (10) (8)

Plates 20 and 21

Tape 8 long stamens and one longer stamen to a wire stem, the same as single fuchsia.

Centre section
1. Form a medium-sized paste cone, suitably coloured.
2. Mark with (10) tool and cut alternate marks. Flatten and round edges.
3. Thin petals with moulding stick against inside of finger; round edges.
4. Fold petals towards centre, overlapping them slightly, moistening sections where petals join.

5. Form three rows of petals, using a slightly larger piece of paste for each successive layer. Turn petals of third row slightly outward.

Back petal section: Form a medium-sized piece of coloured paste into cone and proceed in the same way as for a single fuchsia.

Fuchsia, Cigar (8)

Plate 23

Tape 7 long stamens and one a little longer than the rest to a wire stem.

Centre section:
1. Form a small cone of moulding paste. Insert (8) tool and cut on alternate markings for 4 petals.
2. Pinch, point and flatten each petal; thin out with moulding stick on inside of finger and put aside.

Back petal section
1. Form a larger piece of moulding paste into a cone. Insert (8) tool and cut on alternate markings to form 4 petals.
2. Pinch, point and stretch each petal a little longer than centre section. Thin with moulding stick on inside of finger.
3. Moisten centre of back section and insert centre section, placing the centres of the petals between the outside petals.
4. Moisten stamens and insert into flower. Neaten back with fingers around wire to form a long tapered back.
5. Mould a tiny green bud and place on back.

Buds are long and tapered, slightly bulbous toward tip.

Gardenia (6) (3)

1. Mould 3 tiny yellow curved buds on stamens and tape them to a wire stem (see illustration).
2. Form a cone from a small piece of paste.
3. Mark with (6) tool and cut six petals.
4. Flatten and round edges, thin with moulding tool over side of finger.
5. Place flower on foam block and with (3) tool, using a circular motion, cup each petal.
6. Moisten stem and insert into centre of flower. Neaten back.
7. Make another two rows of petals in a similar manner, using a slightly larger piece of paste for each new row of petals.

8. In assembly, the centres of each succeeding row of petals should align with the joins of the preceding row of petals.

Gypsophila (5)

Plate 5

1. Form a very small piece of paste into a cone, using (5) cone tool on inside of finger until paste is very fine.
2. With scissors cut as many closely spaced petals as possible.
3. With a fine brush moisten base of petals and fold in half, wet base of petals again and fold from both sides to centre.
4. Pull a green hooked wire through centre and neaten back.
5. When dry, dust back of flowers and buds with moss-green petal dust.

Honeysuckle (10)

Plate 7

1. Prepare 6 long stamen pieces with 1 slightly longer, curved over finger and then taped to a wire stem.
2. Form a cone about 2.5 cm long from pale lemon paste.
3. Insert (10) tool and cut alternate markings, with 2 long cuts and 3 short cuts forming 1 long petal and 4 short petals.
4. Round petals.
5. Thin the 4 short petals with moulding stick.
6. Stretch single petal and thin with moulding stick.

7. Turn single petal back.
8. Insert moistened prepared stamens.
9. Dust base of flower with green petal dust.

Japonica (10) (2) (1)

Plate 24

Flowers
1. Tape 3 medium stamens to a wire stem, dip the tips into egg white and then into yellow coloured semolina, making the pistil.
2. Tape 15 more fine yellow stamens around the pistil.
3. Make a medium-sized cone of pink or white moulding paste with the (10) tool and cut on alternate markings for 5 petals.
4. Flatten and round petals.
5. Thin each petal with moulding stick over finger and with (2) tool slightly cup each petal.
6. Moisten stamens and insert into centre. Neaten back.
7. Dust the pink japonica with pink petal dust.
8. Make a green calyx by using the (10) tool and making short cuts on alternate markings.
9. Round and flatten and hollow cone with (1) tool.
10. Moisten inside and add to flower.

Buds
1. Make some the colour of the flower with a green calyx, and some plain green.
2. Using wire and brown florist's tape, make branches, taping on buds and flowers as you go.

Jasmine (10)

1. Form a small cone and mark with (10) tool.
2. Cut alternate markings and round edges.
3. Thin petals with moulding stick.
4. Insert moistened stamen with tip protruding just above centre.
5. Elongate base of flower around the stamen, forming a thin cone.
6. Paint outside of flower pale pink.
7. Paint with green and a touch of brown at base.

Jonquil (6) (5) (7)

Plates 25 and 6

Tape 3 short yellow stamens to a wire stem and put aside.

Petal section
1. Form a cone from a small piece of yellow moulding paste and mark centre with a (6) tool.

2. Cut each mark deeply and stretch each section quite long.
3. Pinch each petal to a point and smooth.
4. Use modelling stick to thin each petal over its full length.
5. Use (7) tool to mark centre of petal over its full length. Put aside.

Centre Section
1. With lemon-yellow moulding paste form a small cone with plain cone tool (5). Roll till thin.
2. With plain cone tool (5) form a cone in the centre of the petal section.
3. Moisten and set trumpet in position. Moisten stem and insert into flower. Neaten back.
4. When dry, colour edge of trumpet an orangey-yellow with liquid colour and bend stem at right angles.

Lilac (8)

1. Form cone from a very small piece of paste. Mark with (8) tool and cut on alternate markings.
2. Pinch each petal to a point and smooth mark out.
3. Thin each petal with roller pin on inside of finger.
4. Insert moistened stamen right down through centre of flower. Neaten back.
5. This flower can be left white or coloured soft lavender.

Lily of the valley (6) (1)

Plate 18

1. Form cone from very small piece of paste and mark with (6) tool.
2. Cut each petal, pinch and smooth pinch out.

(continued on p.49)

On the left, lily of the valley; on the right, English bluebells (page 25)

Plate 1: Easter eggs decorated with flowers without wires (see Helpful Hints, page 61)

Left: Roses and hyacinths (pages 20 and 13)
Right: Orchids, daisies and buttercups (pages 18, 14 and 16)

Plate 2: Single daisies (page 14)

Plate 3: Daffodils (page 17)

Plate 4: Orchids (page 18)

Plate 5: Wired spray of roses and gypsophila (pages 20 and 31)

Plate 6: A moulded shell opening to display jonquils, apple blossom and snowdrops (pages 32, 25 and 22)

Plate 7: Wired sprays of carnations and honeysuckle along with a greeting scroll finish this golden wedding anniversary cake (pages 23 and 31)

Plate 8: White agapanthus (page 25)

Plate 9: Ready for a wedding cake, a moulded bell edged with lace and filled with blue and white agapanthus (page 25)

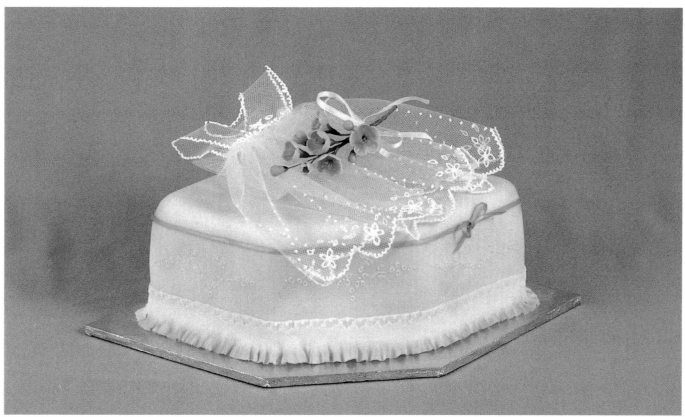

Plate 10: Apple blossom looks attractive lying on a tulle christening gown on a christening cake (page 25)

Plate 11: Bougainvillea (page 25)

Plate 12: A piped lace bell cake top filled with primroses and bouvardia (pages 49 and 26)

Plate 13: On the left, chrysanthemums (page 27); on the right, Carolina yellow jessamine (page 27)

Plate 14: Camellias (page 26)

Plate 15: A cake in the shape of a flowerpot with frilled cyclamen, and an arrangement of non-frilled cyclamen suitable for a cake top (page 27)

Plate 16: Double daisies (page 28)

Plate 17: On the left, roses and eriostemon (pages 20 and 54); on the right, dianthus and eriostemon (pages 29 and 54)

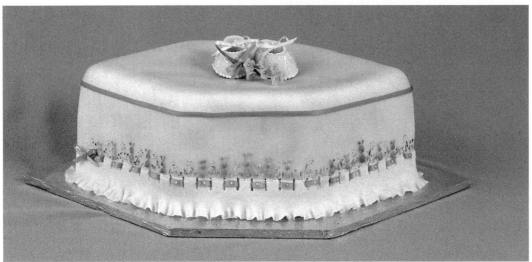

Plate 18 (top): On the left, lily of the valley (page 32); on the right, English lavender (page 29)

Plate 19 (centre): A small spray of forget-me-nots lies next to a pair of moulded bootees on this little boy's christening cake (page 29)

Plate 20: Single and double fuchsias (pages 29 and 30)

Plate 21: Double fuchsia (page 30)

Plate 22: Cigar fuchsia (page 30)

Plate 23: Moulded Christmas bell with rockery succulent, Christmas bells and variegated holly (pages 53 and 50)

Plate 24: Japonica (page 31)

Plate 25: Jonquils (page 32)

Plate 26: Small orchids, primula and bouvardia fill a moulded basket (pages 18, 49 and 26)

Plate 27: Grandma's 80th birthday cake has a wired spray of full-blown roses, bouvardia and gypsophila. Full-blown roses to match were moulded to hold the eight candles

Plate 28: A small Christmas cake suitable for a gift is topped with a spray of Christmas roses and holly

Plate 29: A wired spray of single roses, holly and pine, together with small robins, for a White Christmas theme

Plate 30: This moulded swan makes a lovely cake top for birthday, wedding or christening cakes. Here it has been filled with small roses, hyacinths and violets.

Plate 31: Top, left to right, pine heath and Geraldton wax (pages 56 and 54); bottom, left to right, Mount Lofty correa and boronia (pages 55 and 53)

Plate 32: Yellow jasmine (page 51)

Plate 33: Top, left to right, wild flax, fairy waxflower and wild iris (pages 56, 54 and 56); bottom, left to right, correa, waratah and crowea (pages 53, 56 and 54)

Plate 34: Sixteen different species of Australian native flowers are used in wired sprays for a three-leaf-clover shaped wedding cake

Plate 35: David's 18th birthday cake has a single spray of gum blossom (page 54)

Plate 36: *Pandorea jasminoides* (page 55)

Plate 37: Red roses add the touch of colour needed for the Congratulations cake in black and white. The picture on top is of silhouette work

Plate 38 (left): A display plaque of silhouette work is finished with miniature roses without wire (see Helpful Hints, page 61)

Plate 39: Miniature tooled roses—'Especially for you'

3. Thin with roller pin on inside of finger.
4. With (1) tool form rounded area in centre of flower.
5. Tilt very tip of each petal out.
6. Place yellow moistened stamen in centre.

Orange Blossom No. 1 (5) (10)

Tape one yellow stamen to wire stem.

Centre section
1. Form miniature piece of white paste into cone and with (5) tool roll cone very finely on inside of finger.
2. Cut tiny closely spaced petals.
3. Push moistened stamen through centre and neaten back.

Back petal section
1. Form small piece of paste into cone and mark with (10) tool.
2. Cut alternate markings and ease and pinch petals to 0.5 cm length; smooth pinch marks.
3. Turn petals back and place moistened centre and stem in position.
4. Neaten back.

Orange Blossom No. 2 (10)

1. Tape three small yellow stamens to wire stem.
2. Form a small piece of paste into a cone, mark with (10) tool and cut alternate markings.
3. Pinch petals to a point and stretch to 0.5 cm length.
4. Insert moistened stamens in centre.
5. Turn petals back and neaten back.

Primrose (10)

Plate 12

1. Make a medium-sized cone of lemon-yellow moulding paste using the (10) tool.
2. Make short and long cuts on alternate markings to make 5 heart-shaped petals.
3. Flatten and round each petal, keeping it heart-shaped.
4. Open centre with moulding stick and insert a moistened hooked wire well into the centre.
5. Place a very small ball of green paste down into centre and insert a yellow stamen protruding slightly into green centre.
6. Finish with a small green calyx.

Primula (10) (7)

Plate 26

1. With a small piece of paste form a cone with (10) tool.
2. Make short cuts on alternate markings for 5 petals.
3. Round and flatten petals with roller pin.
4. Press (10) tool in centre again for natural veining.
5. Recess moistened stamen slightly below level of petals.
6. With the edge of (7) tool indent centre of each petal edge to form a heart-shaped petal.
7. Remove excess paste from base and neaten back.
8. When dry, dust centre of flower with pale lemon petal dust.

On the left, rockery succulent (page 51); on the right, a spray of primulas

Rockery Succulent (10)

Plate 24

Tape four stamen stems to a wire stem.

Petals

1. Form small piece of yellow paste into cone and mark with (10) tool.
2. Cut alternate markings, pinch ends and smooth marks out.
3. Thin on inside of finger with roller pin (using it well into the centre).
4. Insert moistened centre. Neaten back.
5. When dry, paint back of flower with red liquid colour.

Calyx

1. Form small cone from piece of light green paste and repeat procedure for making petal section.
2. Turn petals back.
3. Moisten inside of calyx and assemble petals and stem. Neaten back.

Rose, Full-blown (10) (5)

Plate 27

(Detailed instructions for roses appear on pages 20-22.)
1. Tape 20 to 25 fine yellow stamens together on a wire stem.
2. With (10) tool, make a medium cone. Make short cuts on alternate markings for 5 petals.
3. Flatten and round each petal and thin with moulding stick until petals overlap.
4. With (4) tool on edge of finger draw each petal towards centre of flower to curl edge.
5. Moisten prepared stamens and insert into centre. Neaten back.
6. Make another 2 rows of petals in a similar manner, using a slightly larger piece of paste with each new row of petals.
7. In assembly, make sure that the centre of each petal aligns with the joint line of the preceding row of petals.

Rose, Single (10) (4)

Plates 28, 29 and back cover

(Detailed instructions for roses appear on pages 20-22.)
1. Tape about 30 fine yellow stamens together on a wire stem.

2. Spread stamens, moisten, and place a small flat piece of yellow paste in the centre. Allow to dry.
3. With (10) tool, make a medium cone. Make short cuts on alternate markings for 5 petals.
4. Flatten and round each petal and thin with moulding stick until petals overlap.
5. With (4) tool on edge of finger draw each petal towards centre of flower to curl edge.
6. Moisten prepared stamens and insert into centre. Neaten back.
7. When dry, colour flower and add a calyx.
8. Moisten yellow paste of centre with egg white and sprinkle with yellow coloured semolina.

Solomon's Seal (6) (1) (3)

1. Mould a cigar shape about 2.5 cm long; with (6) tool mark and cut each marking.
2. Stretch and pinch petals.
3. Thin petals with moulding stick on inside of finger, working well into centre to hollow out and form tubular flower.
4. With (1) or (3) tool turn the pointed petals inward.
5. Insert the covered wire through the centre.
6. When dry, brush green petal dust on the tips and base of flowers.

On the left, Solomon's seal; on the right, a spray of snowdrops (page 22)

Tuberose (10)

1. Form long cone section from a small piece of moulding paste.

2. Mark with (10) tool and cut fairly deeply.
3. Ease each petal and pinch to a point.
4. Thin with moulding stick.
5. Moisten base of petals, fold petals together and simultaneously fold the ends to meet in the centre.
6. Insert moistened wire stem.
7. Neaten back with finger around wire to form a long tapered back.
8. When dry, paint with cream liquid colour diluted with spirits.

Violet (10)

Plate 30

1. Form a very small cone and use (10) tool to mark it. Cut alternate markings.
2. Stretch, pinch and smooth the top two petals, then thin them with roller pin.
3. Stretch and round edges of the two side petals. Thin with roller pin.
4. Stretch and round edge of bottom 'mouth' petal, thin with roller pin.
5. Mark 3 veins in centre of bottom petal using (10) tool.
6. Dent centre of petal slightly.
7. Insert moistened stamen. Stretch back of flower around stamen and bend stamen.
8. When dry, paint with violet liquid colouring diluted with spirits.

It may be advantageous to form cone slightly thicker one side so that the lower petal can be formed a little larger than the other petals.

Yellow Jasmine (6) (5)

Plate 32

Flower
1. Tape one stamen to a wire stem.
2. Make a medium-sized cone from lemon-yellow moulding paste with (6) tool.
3. Cut in each marking for 6 petals.
4. Flatten and round petals.
5. Thin each petal with moulding stick over finger and give petal natural movement.
6. Open centre with toothpick.
7. Moisten stamen and insert into centre, leaving stamen protruding above centre of flower.
8. Neaten back.
9. Make a second row of 6 petals of same size, opening centre a little with (5) tool.
10. Moisten centre and add to stamen and first row of petals, making sure second row of petals is placed alternately to first.
11. Neaten back by cutting off excess paste and tapering back of flower down stem.

Calyx
1. Using (6) tool and small cone of green paste, cut, pinch, point and flatten.
2. Thin with moulding stick on inside of finger.
3. Moisten and add to flower.
4. Neaten and taper down stem.
5. Dust with lemon petal dust and paint short darker yellow lines radiating from centre.

A moulded Christmas bell filled with a bright and colourful arrangement of rockery
succulent, Christmas bells and variegated holly

Australian Native Flowers

Boronia (8) (1)

Plate 31

1. With a tiny piece of yellow paste form a cone and mark with (8) tool.
2. Cut on alternate markings, pinch to a fine point, and smooth pinch marks.
3. With a curler pin pointed towards the centre of the flower, thin each petal with a side-to-side rolling action on the inside of the index finger.
4. With (1) tool and a stroking action towards the centre, cup each petal (turning it inward).
5. Insert a moistened yellow stamen in the centre.
6. When dry, paint brown on back of petals.

On the left, a spray of Christmas bells; on the right, freesias (page 29)

Christmas Bell (6)

Plate 24

1. Prepare 6 orange-tipped white stamens taped to a wire stem.
2. Form a cigar shape of yellow moulding paste and press one end over a (6) tool.
3. Cut 6 short petals, pinch and flatten them.
4. Thin petals with moulding stick, working well into centre to hollow out and form tubular flower.
5. Insert moistened prepared stamens into centre until stamens are level with top of petals. Neaten back.

Buds are a long cone shape with six small cuts at the end to represent petals.

When dry, brush outside of flowers and buds with red petal dust to base of petals. Tip buds with green petal dust.

Correa (8) (5)

Plate 33

1. Prepare a centre by taping 7 small yellow stamens (about 2.5 cm long) to a wire stem.
2. From a medium-sized piece of moulding paste make a cigar shape.
3. Mark the end with the (8) tool and cut on alternate markings to make 4 petals.
4. Pinch and flatten petals.
5. Thin petals with moulding stick on inside of finger, working well into centre to hollow out and form tubular flower. Turn petals back.
6. Moisten stamens and insert into flower, leaving stamen tips protruding slightly from end. Turn petals back.
7. For the calyx, take a very small piece of moulding paste and form a cone with (5) tool. Moisten inside and put onto flower.

These flowers can be moulded in white moulding paste and coloured when dry with petal dust—cream, pink, red or green.

Crowea (10) (7)

Plate 33

1. Prepare a centre by taping 5 very fine stamen stems to a wire stem.
2. Secure a tiny piece of moulding paste around the taped area and allow to dry.
3. From a very small piece of moulding paste, form a cone using the (10) tool.
4. Cut on alternate markings for 5 petals.
5. Pinch, flatten and thin each petal with a toothpick on inside of finger.
6. Mark a line down centre of each petal with edge of (7) tool.
7. Moisten centre and insert into flower. Neaten back.

These flowers can be moulded with white or pink paste.

Eriostemon (10)

Plate 17

1. Prepare 5 white stamen stems with red-painted tips taped to a wire stem.
2. Form a small cone from paste, insert (10) tool and cut alternate markings.
3. Ease between finger and thumb to lengthen petal.
4. Pinch to a fine point and smooth out pinch mark.
5. Thin petal with roller pin on inside of finger.
6. Place moistened prepared stem in centre.
7. Tint backs of flowers pale pink.

Fairy Waxflower (10)

Plate 33

1. Tape 5 brown-tipped stamens to a wire stem.
2. Form a very small cone from white moulding paste.
3. Insert the (10) tool and cut alternate markings for 5 petals.
4. Pinch and flatten to make pointed petals.
5. Moisten stamens and insert into centre. Neaten back.

Buds are round and very small.

Lightly dust underside of petals and buds with skin-tone petal dust.

Geraldton Wax (10)

Plate 31

1. Form a very small cone from pink moulding paste and mark with (10) tool.
2. Cut on alternate markings.
3. Flatten petals and round edges.
4. Place (10) tool in centre to produce natural veining effect.
5. Insert yellow stamen in centre, letting it protrude beyond the petals.
6. When dry paint burgundy in centre.
7. Pipe small dots of burgundy royal icing at base on the inside of each petal.

Gum Blossom (5)

Plate 35

Centre
1. Wind appropriately coloured cotton around two fingers about 80 times.
2. Remove from fingers and tie each end with fine wire.
3. Cut cotton through middle. This forms two centres.
4. Cover wire with Parafilm tape.

Flower
1. Take a medium-sized piece of green paste and form a cone.
2. Hollow out centre of cone with the (5) tool.
3. Moisten inside of cone and pull prepared centre through.
4. Make a very small ball of green paste and put on to a hooked wire. Insert through cotton centre, leaving it protruding above cotton to form the pistil.

5. Moisten tips of cotton with egg white and dip in gelatine. This gives the effect of pollen.

8. When dry, dust outside with red petal dust and green on the tips of the petals.

Kurrajong (10)

1. Prepare 5 white stamens tipped in burgundy colour and taped to a wire stem.
2. Form a small cone and mark with (10) tool.
3. Cut 5 short petals on alternate markings.
4. Stretch petals, pinch to point and smooth.
5. Thin with roller pin over side of finger.
6. Insert prepared stamens and neaten back.
7. When dry paint back of flower burgundy.

Left to right: violets (page 51), a spray of kurrajong (above) and rockery succulent (p.50)

Native Heath (10)

1. Tape 5 stamens to a wire stem.
2. With a small amount of pale pink paste form a long narrow cone.
3. Mark with (10) tool and cut alternate markings.
4. Pinch petals to a fine point, smooth out pinch marks.
5. Work roller pin down into centre of flower to form a tubular flower.
6. Tilt tips of petals slightly outward.
7. Insert moistened stamen in centre.

Left to right: native heath (above); a spray of eriostemon (page 54) and forget-me-nots (page 29)

Mount Lofty Correa (8) (5)

Plate 31

1. Prepare a centre by taping 5 small yellow stamens and 1 stamen stem to a wire stem. The stamen stem should be longer than the stamens.
2. From a small piece of moulding paste make a slim cigar shape.
3. Mark the end with the (8) tool and cut on alternate markings making 4 petals.
4. Pinch and flatten petals.
5. Thin petals with toothpick on inside of finger, working well into centre to hollow out and form tubular flower. Do not turn petals back.
6. Moisten stamen stems and insert into flower.
7. For calyx, take a very small piece of moulding paste and form a cone with the (5) tool. Moisten inside and put onto flower.

Pandorea Jasminoides (10) (5)

Plate 36

1. Tape 4 white stamens and 1 longer one to a wire stem.
2. Prepare a medium-sized cone from very pale pink moulding paste with the (10) tool.
3. Cut on alternate markings for 5 petals.
4. Flatten and round petals.
5. Thin each petal with moulding stick over finger to give petal natural movement.
6. Open up centre with moulding stick or (5) tool to make a tube-shaped flower.
7. Insert moistened stamens into centre.
8. Turn 2 petals back.
9. When dry, dust or paint centre throat with burgundy colour.

Pine Heath (10)

Plate 31

1. Prepare a centre by taping 1 yellow stamen to a wire stem.
2. From a small piece of lemon yellow moulding paste make a slim cigar shape.
3. Mark the end with the (10) tool and make very short cuts on alternate markings for 5 petals.
4. Pinch and flatten petals.
5. Thin petals with toothpick on inside of finger, working well into centre to hollow out and form a tubular flower.
6. Turn the tiny petals back.
7. Moisten stamen centre and insert into flower.
8. Use green stamen stems for pine-like leaves.
9. When dry, brush petal tips with green petal dust.

Waratah (8)

Plate 33 and front cover

Centre
1. Using red moulding paste make a rounded pyramid about the size of a thumb nail and attach to a hooked wire.
2. Allow to dry.
3. Using white royal icing and No. 2 piping tube, pipe dots on top of the centre and continue down the sides, drawing the dots down so that they stand out. Continue to about two-thirds the way down. This makes the individual flowerets. Allow to dry. (Look closely at colour picture for the effect required.)

Flower
1. Make a medium cone of red moulding paste using (8) tool.
2. Make long cuts in each marking.
3. Pinch each petal to a point, flatten and stretch.
4. Thin with a moulding stick.
5. Moisten back of centre and insert into petals, twisting them to give a natural appearance.
6. Make a second row of petals and add to flower.
7. Paint over centre and petals with red colouring.
8. When dry touch top of flower with a little moss-green petal dust.

Wild Flax (10)

Plate 33

1. Prepare a centre by taping 5 short, pale blue stamens (one slightly longer than the others) to a wire stem.
2. Secure a tiny piece of moulding paste around the taped area and allow to dry. With lemon colouring, paint very fine stripes vertically around moulding paste cover.
3. With a small piece of pale blue moulding paste form a cone using the (10) tool. Cut on alternate markings for 5 petals.
4. Stretch and round each petal and thin with modelling stick.
5. Take moistened centre and insert into flower.
6. When dry, paint very fine short blue lines radiating from the centre of the flower.

Wild Iris (6) (7)

Plate 33

1. Tape 3 short yellow stamens to a wire stem and bend each stamen out.
2. Prepare a medium-sized cone from pale lavender-blue moulding paste with (6) tool.
3. Cut on alternate markings for 3 petals.
4. Pinch each petal to a point. Flatten and stretch.
5. Thin with moulding stick.
6. Mark a vein down centre of each petal with (7) tool.
7. Insert moistened stamen centre and neaten back.
8. Touch each stamen tip with a little egg white and then sprinkle with yellow coloured semolina.
9. Finally dust petals with darker lavender petal dust.

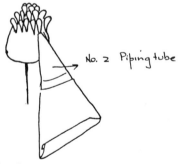

No. 2 Piping tube

The flowerets in the centre of the waratah

Leaves and Arrangements

Leaves (2) (7)

1. Take a moistened wire stem and push about two-thirds of the way into a cone-shaped piece of paste. Size of cone will depend on size of leaf required.

2. Using a modelling stick, roll out paste, working from the centre outwards. Leave the paste thicker over the wire.

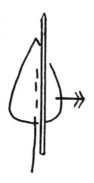

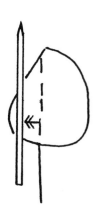

3. Cut out a leaf using a leaf cutter or pattern. Place the leaf on a piece of sponge foam and run the (2) tool around the edge.

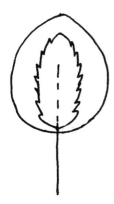

4. Use the edge of the (7) tool to add veins.

5. Leave to dry.

Colour by brushing with petal dust or diluted liquid colour.

Leaf Patterns

Patterns can be made from real leaves.

The plastic lids of margarine containers make good pattern templates.

Daisy Leaf

Small Holly Leaf

Large Holly Leaf

Narrow Leaf Pattern

Small Rose Leaf

Medium Rose Leaf

**Large Gum
Leaf Pattern**

Large Rose Leaf

Rose leaf patterns can be used for any leaf that has a similar shape.

Arrangement of Small Flowers

Cut Parafilm or floral tape into thirds lengthwise. Using the narrow lengths gives a neater finish to wired arrangements.

Small flowers, e.g. hyacinths and primula, are arranged in small sprays by taping together 3 flowers and 1 or 2 buds as shown in the diagram.

These small sprays are then used in this way for larger floral arrangements.

Small Flower Sprays

Basic 18 cm Floral Arrangement

1. Using an already cut length of tape, join together 3 small leaves and a small spray of flowers, winding and stretching the tape around the stems.

2. Continue as in previous step, increasing the size of the leaves, sprays and flowers and keeping each addition evenly spaced.

The junction of the stem of the 10th addition will become the PIVOT POINT.

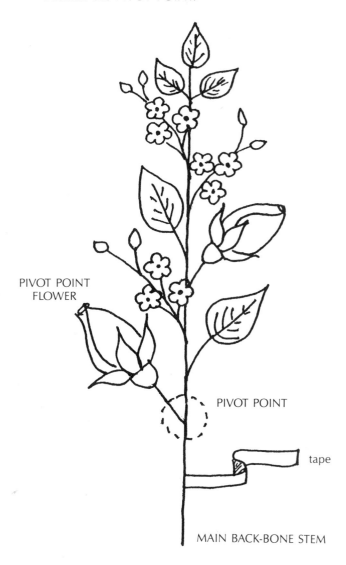

PIVOT POINT FLOWER

PIVOT POINT

tape

MAIN BACK-BONE STEM

3. Place the stem of a larger flower, the FOCAL FLOWER, through the pivot point. Bend the focal flower stem back along the BACK-BONE STEM of arrangement. The focal flower sits higher than other flowers.

    The next flower to be added is the LENGTH FLOWER.

    All further flowers, sprays and leaves must have the stems going through the pivot point and folded back along the main back-bone stem, taping securely.

Finish and neaten back-bone stem by cutting the wire stems back so that they do not show beyond the length flower. Cover neatly with tape.

Extra flowers, sprays, leaves and ribbon can be added to this basic arrangement if required.

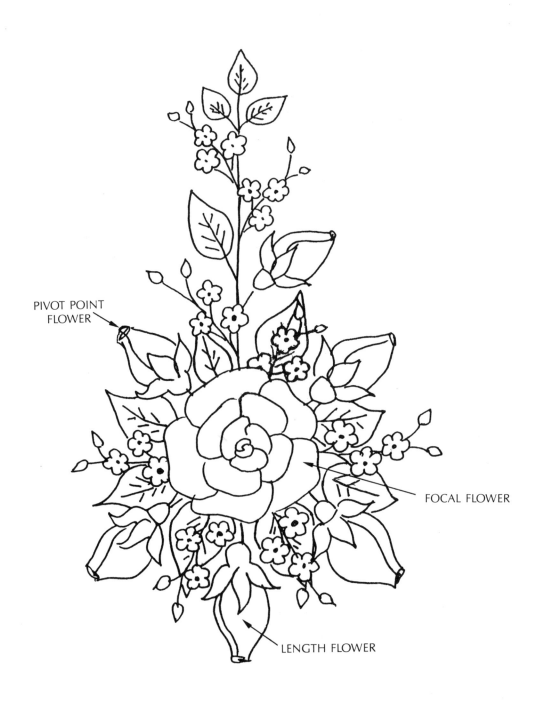

PIVOT POINT
FLOWER

FOCAL FLOWER

LENGTH FLOWER

Helpful Hints

1. It is so much easier to make sugar flowers using the real flower as a guide. If you haven't got time to copy one when they are flowering, put the real flower in a plastic jar, cover with plastic wrap and place in freezer.

2. A lovely frill can be achieved by using the (2) tool and simply rolling the ball tool around the edge of the paste. This frill is nice for petals and leaves where a frilled edge is needed.

3. The (1) (2) (3) and (4) tools can be used for thinning and cupping petals. Place petal or leaf on a piece of sponge foam and use tool in a circular action on centre.

4. Instead of fingering petals and leaves, put them on foam and run the ball tool (2) around the edge. This takes away the cut edge look and adds natural movement to petals and leaves.

5. For veining—use the (7) tool for single veins and the (10) tool where more veins are needed.

6. The tools can be used in other crafts, e.g. bread dough jewellery, ceramics and moulded clay work.

7. Small roses can be made without wire for use on plaques, Easter eggs, etc. Make the rose as described in the Rose instructions on pages 20-22, pulling out the starter while petals are still wet. Set rose aside to dry. The same starter can be used again and again.